DON'T JUS^T. ᴇᴀ..

Inspiring foods to eat and stay healthy- preventing Cardiovascular diseases,Stroke, Obesity, Diabetes, and Improving Healthy Digestion.

By

Dr. Ashley Mayer

TABLE OF CONTENTS

INTRODUCTION 3

CHAPTER 1 7

THE WAY YOU CONSIDER FOOD 7

CHAPTER 2 13

HONEY AND WHOLE GRAIN 13

CHAPTER 3 27

NUTS 27

1. Peanuts 28

2. Almonds 31

3. Pistachios 33

4. Cashews 35

5. Walnuts 36

CHAPTER 4 41

LEAN MEAT 41

6. Hazelnuts 43

1. Chicken: 46

2. Turkey: 47

3. Fish: 48

4. Pork Loin: 49

CHAPTER 5 53

FRUITS AND VEGETABLES 53

CHAPTER 6 69

BENEFITS OF HEALTHY EATING 69

1. More Economically Sound 69

2. Your health improves 70

4. A more active lifestyle 71

5. Optimal Social Life 72

6. Cardiovascular health 72

7. Strong teeth and bones 73

CONCLUSION 75

INTRODUCTION

Simply put, the body has two very different and complex systems for producing energy. Because energy is essential to human activity and survival, the two-energy Each style relies on the other for support. This book demonstrates What foods provide you with the most energy?

It happens so frequently that we decide to continue with a health regimen.

and physical fitness program with zeal and, most likely, fanfare too; however, during the first week of implementing the plan,

Everything comes to a halt. Why do we fail to stick to our diets? plans for morning jogging, plans for physical exercise that we create? And what can we do to ensure that we stick to our plans, both for our own sake and for the sake of those who rely on us?

Are you eating simply to satisfy your hunger or to improve your health?

Are your taste buds satisfied?

Or are you eating to improve your command your existence?

This Book will show you how to improve your life much better simply by making it a point to eat correctly.

Energy is required for a variety of functions such as growth maintenance, daily activities, exercise, and a variety of other movements or functions that are frequently overlooked. These are shared by both energy systems.

In today's world, few health and fitness plans are successful. What is the cause of their alarming failure rate? The world today is far less healthy than it was two decades ago. Much of this is due to people's changing eating habits. The aerobic system is the primary and first to be used energy system. This system requires a lot from the rest of the body in order for the muscles to function properly. This demand typically increases the rate and depth of breathing as well as blood supply, owing to the corresponding increase in heart rate.

When the body requires more energy and this cannot be met due to the increased need for more oxygen, the body system switches to anaerobic energy. This system can generate energy without the use of oxygen. All of this energy is generated by the appropriate or correct consumption of foods. Everyone's energy levels are determined by the foods they eat. Muscle fatigue typically occurs when all energy sources are depleted, which can be attributed to a number of factors, the most compelling of which is the type of foods consumed.

CHAPTER 1

THE WAY YOU CONSIDER FOOD

The most important thing you need to keep your health and fitness program going – even more important than an instructor or a doctor – is your own motivation. You must be determined to investigate the situation. So you're a little overweight and want to lose a few pounds. No gym instructor in the world will be able to help you if you do not take the necessary steps to maintain a healthy diet and adhere to a regular exercise regimen. Even if you're sick and seeking treatment, no doctor will be able to assist you if you're not committed to following the treatment plan, whether it's taking medication at the appropriate time or abstaining from certain foods. There are several food categories that produce various beneficial elements for the human body system, and it is useful to know which ones create or enhance energy generating sources. As a result, this knowledge should assist the individual in selecting the appropriate types of foods. The aerobic system works by breaking down the carbohydrates, fatty acids, and amino acids in the foods we eat, whereas the anaerobic system releases energy from the foods we store in our bodies, usually during periods of intense activity. If we hear about diets or gym plans failing all around us, it's usually not their fault.It's usually the fault of the people who made a big deal about going through these plans, telling all their friends and coworkers about it, and then didn't follow through on it. Individuals who abandon the exercise or diet program in the middle do not see the benefits, and everyone blames the plan. What the world requires today is motivation, not a new health or fitness program or diet. It takes the right kind of mindset to see through whatever plan they have chosen to the end. If they can accomplish this, most lifestyle-related health issues will be rendered obsolete. And we don't have to travel to the ends of the earth to find this motivation. The motivation is already within us; we just need to find it and use it. A generation ago, people would not have dreamed of eating whatever junk food they could get their hands on. Nowadays, we do it so casually.

"I'm hungry," in most cases, means "I want a burger or a hot dog, probably with chips and cola on the side." And "I'm on a diet" means "I'm on a chemically laced pill that will satisfy my hunger while depriving my body of vitamins." It's no surprise that we have so many health problems today. Our health is a reflection of what we eat. The sorry state in which we find ourselves is not an individual issue; it is a global one. The entire world eats incorrectly. Six out of every ten people in the United States are overweight, and that number is expected to rise to eight out of ten by 2024.

Are we seriously considering this? We're not. Even as you read this Book, you're probably snacking on some chips. Do you realize that the money you spent on that package, which is filling your stomach with some of the most toxic chemicals known to humanity, could have instead fed an undernourished child in the remote area? But it's not just about being charitable. It is also about ourselves. Yes, we must be selfish. With such dismal health statistics, aren't we doomed? We're clearly not eating properly. We must be prepared for whatever excess baggage that brings, including obesity and other ill health consequences. So, the next time you see a program that has failed or is receiving a lot of criticism, remember that it isn't because the program is on shaky ground. In most cases, it is because people began with good intentions but then did not adhere to the program as strictly as they should have.

YOUR MENTALITY ABOUT FOOD

So far, our eating habits have been disastrous. Things will not improve unless we take stock of the situation and take control of the situation. The most important factor is awareness. We must learn which foods are good for us and which are not. We must return to training to determine which nutrients your body requires and in what quantities. Then we must devise a dietary regimen for ourselves and our loved ones in order to eat healthier. We must eliminate all harmful foods - sugars, fats, and carbohydrates, which we do not desire - and replace them with foods that may benefit our health. I understand if this sounds too preachy. But that is the only respite we have. We'll never be able to improve if we keep eating Oreos. But there is still hope. There are a lot of foods out there that are just as tasty as those horrible junk foods, but we don't know about them yet. These are the foods we don't know about because we don't like them or don't know how to prepare them, but a healthy cookbook can help you understand various interesting ways to cook healthy. Even if you stick to the same diet, you can create some really delicious healthy dishes. Yes, everything is possible. You can significantly alter your eating habits while also paying attention to your palate.

The truth is that the weight loss industry has played a significant role in the decline of the developed human race. They need to keep selling their Atkins and Jenny Craigs and Zones and Medi-fasts, so the media never tells you how you can take matters into your own hands. They show us glitzy before-and-after pictures of a person with a foot-long sub and then the same guy with six pack abs and tell us that the diet allowed them to achieve that. However, if we put our heads together, we could easily do that as well, without having to spend thousands of dollars on those diets. And what should we do? Control what we eat. Engage in some physical activity.

Is that too much to ask of you? Don't we owe it to our bodies, which have served us so well over the years? Do we not owe it to ourselves and our loved ones?

CHAPTER 2

HONEY AND WHOLE GRAIN

Honey has been proven to be the one sustaining power behind the energy circle over the years. It continues to be unrivaled in its energy producing entity, benefiting the human body in a variety of ways. Honey is nature's most natural source of energy. It also serves as an effective immune system booster, as well as a natural remedy for a variety of ailments.

Energy is critical to the natural flow of any human being's daily life cycle. Finding energy sources that are both consistent and healthy is therefore critical to staying fit and happy.Honey's natural benefits are widely recognized and accepted. Aside from its delicious flavor, honey is a natural source of carbohydrate, which is an energy source for improving performance, endurance, and reducing muscle fatigue. This is especially beneficial to athletes. The sugar content of honey aids in the prevention of fatigue during exercise sessions and training sessions for sports enthusiasts. These sugars are divided into glucose and fructose, which serve different but complementary functions.

The glucose in honey is generally absorbed at a faster rate and provides an immediate energy boost, whereas the fructose works at a slower rate and provides a more sustainable and prolonged energy dispersal. When it comes to blood sugar levels in the body, honey has been shown to help keep them relatively constant. Consuming honey is not a difficult exercise because it is a pleasant food product that is natural in its form. People of all ages are generally eager to consume honey in any of its associated forms. It's even popular among kids. The energy provided by a small amount of honey consumed daily helps children cope with the physical strains of daily school activities and sports commitments. Consuming a small amount of honey on a daily basis can help adults maintain their energy levels during a long day at work. Making sandwiches with honey and other fillings is one way to make a tasty snack. A freshly toasted slice of bread with honey on top is also a tasty breakfast option. Using honey instead of sugar in drinks is strongly encouraged.

Most people nowadays want a quick fix for their energy needs, which usually comes in the form of unhealthy sports drinks, coffee, and refined carbohydrates like sugar and white bread. Though these produce the desired increased energy levels, it should be noted that this energy is relatively fleeting, and the tiredness that follows is usually more acutely felt. Consuming some form of whole grains is thus not only a better option, but also much healthier. Whole grains provide energy in a more complex form that degrades over a longer period of time. This then serves as the foundation for maintaining energy levels for longer periods of time.

Because of their more complex composition, whole grains contain a variety of beneficial elements such as minerals, vitamins, phytonutrients, and fiber, which are also high in fiber. Including whole grain ingredients in any dish almost always completes or enhances the flavor. Whole grains include wheat, oat, barley, maize, brown rice, faro, spelt, emmer, einkorn, rye, millet, buckwheat, and many others.

These can then be processed into whole wheat flour, whole wheat bread, whole wheat pasta, rolled oats or oat groats, triticale flour, popcorn, and teff flour. Consuming whole grains on a regular basis can help reduce the risk of heart disease, lower cholesterol levels, protect against many types of cancer, and aid in weight management. Whole grains should not be confused with their less refined "cousin." Though refined grains have some advantages, whole grain alternatives are always preferable.

BENEFITS OF HONEY AND WHOLE GRAIN

1. High in fiber and nutrients

Whole grains contain a variety of essential nutrients. Fiber is one of them. The bran contains the majority of the fiber in whole grains.

Vitamins. Whole grains are high in B vitamins, such as niacin, thiamine, and folate minerals. They also have a high mineral content, including zinc, iron, magnesium, and manganese.

Protein. Per serving, whole grains contain several grams of protein.

Antioxidants. Many of the compounds found in whole grains act as antioxidants. Phytic acid, lignans, ferulic acid, and sulfur compound are examples of these. Compounds derived from plants Whole grains contain a variety of plant compounds that aid in disease prevention. Polyphenols, stanols, and sterols are examples of these.

2. Reduce your chances of developing heart disease.

Whole grains have many health benefits, including lowering your risk of heart disease, which is the leading cause of death worldwide.

According to a review of ten studies, eating three 1-ounce (28-gram) servings of whole grains daily may reduce your risk of heart disease by 22%.

Similarly, a 10-year study of 17,424 adults found that those who consumed the most whole grains in relation to total carb intake had a 47% lower risk of heart disease. According to the researchers, heart-healthy diets should include more whole grains and fewer refined grains. Most studies group different types of whole grains together, making it difficult to separate the benefits of individual foods.

3. Reduce your chances of having a stroke.

Whole grains may also reduce your risk of having a stroke. In a meta-analysis of six studies involving nearly 250,000 people, those who consumed the most whole grains had a 14% lower risk of stroke than those who consumed the fewest. Furthermore, whole grains contain compounds that can lower your risk of stroke, such as fiber, vitamin K, and antioxidants. Whole grains are also suggested in the DASH and Mediterranean diets, which may help reduce your risk of stroke.

4. Reduce your chances of becoming obese.

Consuming fiber-rich foods can help you feel full and avoid overeating. This is one of the reasons why high-fiber diets are suggested for weight loss. Whole grains and products made from them are more filling than refined grains and may reduce your risk of obesity, according to research.

In fact, a review of 15 studies involving nearly 120,000 people found that eating three servings of whole grains per day was associated with a lower BMI and less belly fat. Another study that looked at research from 1965 to 2010 discovered that whole-grain cereal and cereal with added bran were linked to a slightly lower risk of obesity. Decades of research have linked whole grains to a lower risk of obesity.

5. Reduce your chances of developing type 2 diabetes.

Consuming whole grains instead of refined grains may reduce your risk of type 2 diabetes.

A review of 16 studies concluded that substituting whole grains for refined grains and eating at least two servings of whole grains per day could reduce your risk of diabetes. This is due, in part, to the fact that fiber-rich whole grains can aid in weight control and the prevention of obesity, which is a risk factor for diabetes.

Furthermore, research has linked whole grain consumption to lower fasting blood sugar levels and improved insulin sensitivity.

This could be due to magnesium, a mineral found in whole grains that aids in carbohydrate metabolism and has been linked to insulin sensitivity.

6. Encourage healthy digestion

Whole grain fiber can help with digestion in a variety of ways.

First, fiber adds bulk to stools and reduces the risk of constipation.

Second, certain types of fiber in grains function as prebiotics. This means they aid in the feeding of your beneficial gut bacteria, which is essential for digestive health. Whole grains help support healthy digestion by providing bulk to stools and feeding your beneficial gut bacteria.

Honey is sometimes used to treat digestive issues like diarrhea, though research on its effectiveness is limited. However, it may have potential as a treatment for Helicobacter pylori (H. pylori), a common cause of stomach ulcers.

It also contains beneficial prebiotics, which feed the good bacteria that live in the intestines, which are important not only for digestion but also for overall health.

7. An excellent source of antioxidants

Raw honey is rich in plant chemicals that act as antioxidants. Some honeys contain the same amount of antioxidants as fruits and vegetables. Antioxidants help to protect your cells from free radical damage.
Free radicals accelerate aging and may contribute to the development of chronic diseases such as cancer and heart disease. Polyphenols, antioxidant compounds found in raw honey, have anti-inflammatory properties that may help protect against a variety of oxidative stress-related conditions, according to research.

8. Nutritional value of raw honey

The nutritional value of raw honey varies depending on its origin and other factors. One tablespoon of raw honey, or 21 grams, contains 64 calories and 17 grams of sugar. Raw honey also contains trace amounts of the micro nutrients (or vitamins and minerals) listed below:
calcium
Magnesium

manganese

pantothenic

acid niacin

phosphorous

potassium

Riboflavin

Zinc.

9. Heals injuries

According to a 2018 review of studies, honey has antimicrobial properties. According to a 2017 review of studies, honey, propolis, and royal jelly may have potential health benefits for microbial inhibition and wound healing.

Keep in mind that the honey used in research is medical grade, which means it has been inspected and is sterile. It's not a good idea to treat cuts with store-bought honey. Before using honey for medical purposes, always consult with your doctor.

10. Anti-fungal and Anti-bacterial qualities

According to studies, propolis in raw honey has antifungal and antibacterial properties. Raw honey has the potential to be used for both internal and external treatments. The effectiveness of honey as an antibacterial or antifungal varies depending on the honey, but some varieties are being researched for specific therapeutic uses such as Candida-associated infections.

11. Sore throat and cough relief

Honey is an old sore throat remedy that relieves pain and can aid in coughing. When a cold virus strikes, mix it into hot tea with lemon.

Though more research is needed, a review of studies published in 2021 suggested that honey may be superior to other forms of treatment for the treatment of upper respiratory tract infections.

According to a 2016 study, the antibacterial and anti-inflammatory properties can also help with a sore throat.

12. Benefits for the Brain

There may even be some cognitive benefits to raw honey. The polyphenols in honey may be able to counter inflammation in the hippocampus, the part of the brain involved in memory.

Many parts of the body, including brain health, can benefit from antioxidant and anti-inflammatory effects.

CHAPTER 3

NUTS

In botany, a nut is a dry hard fruit that does not split open at maturity to release its single seed. A nut is similar to an achene, but it grows from more than one carpel (female reproductive structure), is often larger, and has a tough woody wall. True nuts include the chestnut, hazelnut, and acorn. Many edible oily seeds, especially those with a hard shell, are commonly referred to as "nuts." Many of these culinary nuts are the seeds of drupe fruits, such as walnuts, pistachios, almonds, and coconuts. The peanut is a legume, and the Brazil nut is a seed from a capsule fruit. Nuts are an excellent source of healthy fats, fiber, and other nutrients. Each nut has its own set of nutritional benefits.

Nuts are a good source of plant-based protein. According to a 2017 review study a diet rich in nuts may help prevent risk factors for some chronic diseases, such as inflammation.

SIX OF THE HEALTHIEST NUTS

The list below ranks six different types of nuts in terms of protein content and discusses their other nutritional benefits. Each nutrient measurement is for 100 grams (g) of raw nut.

1. Peanuts

Eating peanuts is an excellent way for people to increase their protein intake. Peanuts are widely available and contain a variety of essential nutrients.

Although peanuts are technically a legume, which means they belong to a specific plant family, most people consider them to be a nut.

Polyphenols, antioxidants, flavonoids, and amino acids are all found in peanuts. All of these components have been shown in studies to be beneficial to human health. According to the United States Department of Agriculture's (USDA) nutrient database, 100 g of peanuts contains 567 calories and the following amounts of other nutrients:

Protein: 25.80 g

Fat: 49.24 g

Carbohydrate: 16.13 g

Fiber: 8.50 g

Sugar: 4.72 g

Peanuts' fats are mostly monounsaturated and polyunsaturated fatty acids (PUFAs), with a small amount of saturated fat.

There are also numerous minerals in 100 g of peanuts, including the following:

Milligrams calcium :92 (mg)

Iron: 4.58 mg

Magnesium: 168 mg

Phosphorus: 376 mg

Potassium: 705 mg

Peanuts also have the advantage of being less expensive than many other nut varieties.

Peanuts

2. Almonds

Almonds have grown in popularity in recent years, and they are now widely available in a variety of stores. They have slightly less protein than peanuts but compensate with other nutrients.

Almonds may be the ideal snack for those looking for a protein-rich alternative to potato chips or pretzels.

Each 100 g of almonds contains 579 calories and has the following nutritional profile, according to the USDA:

Carbohydrate: 21.55 g

Protein: 21.15 g

 Fiber: 12.50g

Glucose: 4.35 g

Almonds contain a large amount of monounsaturated fats. Additionally, almonds contain many vitamins and minerals, including:

Calcium 270 mg

Iron- 3.71 mg

Magnesium- 270 mg

Phosphorous- 481 mg

Potassium- 733 mg

Vitamin E- 25.63 mcg

Almonds nuts

3. Pistachios

Pistachios are high in protein and other essential nutrients. They also contain beneficial fatty acids and antioxidants. The popular green nut is actually a seed of the pistachio tree, but people mistake it for a nut because of its appearance and feel.

A study published in Nutrition Today found that eating pistachios lowers blood pressure and improves endothelial function, potentially lowering the risk of heart disease.

According to the USDA database, 100 g of pistachios contains 560 calories as well as the following nutrients:

protein: 20.16 g

fat: 45.32 g

carbohydrate: 27.17 g

fiber: 10.60 g

sugar: 7.66 g

The majority of the fat in pistachios is made up of beneficial monounsaturated fatty acids and PUFAs.

Pistachios contain 1,025 mg of potassium per 100 g, which is a significant amount despite having fewer minerals than some other nuts.

Pistachios also contain the following important vitamins and minerals:

calcium: 105 mg

iron: 3.92 mg

magnesium: 121 mg

phosphorous: 490 mg

Pistachios nuts

4. Cashews

Cashews are a great addition to many dishes and snacks because of their creamy texture.

100 g of cashews have 553 calories and the following nutrients, according to the USDA:

protein: 18.22 g

fat: 43.85 g

carbohydrate: 30.19 g

fiber: 3.30 g

sugar: 5.91 g

In cashews, monounsaturated fats make up the majority of the fats.

Cashews contain essential vitamins and minerals like:

calcium: 37 mg

iron: 6.68 mg

magnesium: 292 mg

phosphorous: 593 mg

potassium: 660 mg

Cashew nuts

5. Walnuts

Despite having fewer carbohydrates than many other nuts, walnuts have more calories than some of them. The extremely high fat content is the cause of the high calorie count.

However, the majority of the fats in walnuts are PUFAs, which may have a number of health advantages.

Walnuts are a good source of protein and other nutrients, though they are best known for their healthy fat content.

The USDA lists walnuts as having 654 calories per 100 g and also having:

protein: 15.23 g

fat: 65.21 g

carbohydrate: 13.71 g

fiber: 6.7 g

sugar: 2.61 g

Compared to other nuts, walnuts have a slightly lower mineral content.

calcium: 98 mg

iron: 2.91 mg

magnesium: 158 mg

phosphorous: 346 mg

potassium: 441 mg

Walnuts

CHAPTER 4

LEAN MEAT

You may have heard that protein helps speed up metabolism and decrease feelings of hunger. Perhaps you've also heard about how it keeps you fuller longer, preventing unneeded binges. If you're dieting to lose weight, you may have heard your friends and trainers stress how important protein is. You may have heard that protein helps speed up metabolism and decrease feelings of hunger. Perhaps you've also heard about how it keeps you fuller longer, preventing unneeded binges. But what if we told you that even all of this knowledge is insufficient to begin a diet high in protein? Protein is a necessary component of any diet for losing weight, but the type of protein you should consume is just as crucial! Lean protein can help in this situation.

The most popular sources of lean protein you can eat a lot of include skinless chicken and turkey, non-fat dairy, fish, shellfish, tofu, and other soy products. And among these, the meats from animal sources are grouped together under the heading "Lean Meat."

What is lean meat? And Why Is It More Preferable to Red Meat?

Lean meat is a general term for "white" meat, poultry, or fish that contains fewer calories and fat than its fatty red counterparts.

Shalini Manglani, a nutritionist and wellness specialist located in Bangalore, claims that lean meats like chicken and fish have less fat than red meats like lamb, mutton, and pork. Lean meat is preferable if one is concerned about consuming too much fat or has been told to avoid it. Lean meat and red meat both contain about 7 gms of protein per 30 gm serving. A meal should ideally consist of two pieces of meat and a side of veggies or grains. The portion size may differ based on a person's height and weight.

In comparison to poultry, fish, and vegetable proteins like beans and lentils, red meat has higher levels of cholesterol and saturated fat. Your blood cholesterol levels can be raised by cholesterol and saturated fat, which, in more severe circumstances, may result in cardiac conditions. When following a healthy weight reduction diet, chicken and fish are one of your best allies because they are high in protein and contain less saturated fat than the majority of red meat. In addition, poultry is a significant source of selenium, B vitamins (especially B3) and B6 as well as choline. Selenium has been connected to a boost in immunity and a reduction in cellular free radical activity.

6. Hazelnuts

Hazelnuts are a favorite ingredient in sweet foods because of their distinctive flavor. Compared to other nuts, hazelnuts have a lower protein content, but they may make up for it in other ways. Hazelnuts may help lower cholesterol, according to a study that was published in the Journal of Clinical Lipidology. According to the USDA database, 100 g of hazelnuts have 628 calories and the following nutrients:

protein: 14.95 g

fat: 60.75 g

carbohydrate: 16.70 g

fiber: 9.7 g

sugar: 4.34 g

Due to their high protein and fat content, hazelnuts resemble walnuts more than any other kind of nut.

Hazelnuts contain mostly monounsaturated fats, but they also contain some polyunsaturated and saturated fats. Additionally, hazelnuts contain the following:

calcium: 114 mg

iron: 4.70 mg

magnesium: 163 mg

phosphorous: 290 mg

potassium: 680 mg

Hazelnuts

Consuming nuts is good for your health because they may shield you from conditions like heart disease and other risk factors. It is possible to consume too many nuts, though. Nuts contain a lot of calories, so eating a lot of them throughout the day can cause people to consume more calories than they intended to. Regularly doing so might result in weight gain.

Nuts contain a lot of healthy fats, which are beneficial to the body when consumed in moderation but can have negative effects if consumed in excess. Roasted, salted nuts can contribute to the diet at least as much sodium as other salty snacks. Anyone who consumes salted nuts should read the label carefully to determine how much sodium they are consuming. Nuts that are raw or dry-roasted are healthier options.

Best sources of lean meat

1. Chicken:

One of the best sources of lean protein is said to be chicken. "Chicken is packed with lean protein that helps you stay full for a longer time since protein helps you burn fat more effectively," says macrobiotic nutritionist and health practitioner Shilpa Arora. Chicken that has been reared organically or on a local farm is preferred. For best results, grill, stir-fry, or include them into stews.

One of the best sources of lean protein is said to be chicken.

2. Turkey:

Turkey is another another amazing poultry product that is rich in lean protein. Over 133 grams of protein are present in one pound of light turkey flesh that has been roasted. The always adaptable turkey never lets you down whether you use it in salads, soups, or sandwiches.

Turkey meat is loaded with lean protein

3. Fish:

Salmon, trout, sardines, tuna, and mackerel are just a few of the fresh, fatty fish that are included on the list of lean meats. In addition to protein, fish is high in the brain-healthy Omega-3 fatty acids and vitamin D.

Fresh salmon fish is a good source of lean meat

4. Pork Loin:

It turns out that not all cuts of the red, fatty meat of the pork are unhealthy. Pork loin chops and pork tenderloin are lean pork cuts that are a good source of your daily protein need. Pork has only 2 grams of saturated fat, roughly 23 grams of protein, and a ton of B vitamins in an amount of 85 grams.

Pork fatty red meat

Even while preparing these lean meats, be careful to choose your cooking method. Grill rather than deep-fry. Or use fresh herbs in baking rather than relying on mayo for flavor!

Protein is a very vital component of the basic structural and functional development of every cell nourishment and production and is generally higher and purer in lean meats.

Essential amino acids, notably sulfur amino acids, are also abundant in lean meats. When compared to digestion rates, animal proteins function more quickly than those found in beans and whole grains.

Iron can also be found in lean meat. Because iron deficiency is gradual, it frequently goes undetected until anemia has set in.

CHAPTER 5

FRUITS AND VEGETABLES

Your daily diet should include plenty of fruits and vegetables. They are nutritious by nature and include vitamins and minerals that can support your overall well-being. They can aid in illness prevention as well.

Eating more fruits and vegetables as part of a balanced, healthy diet and an active lifestyle will benefit the majority of Australians. Fruits and vegetables come in a wide range of kinds, and there are several ways to cook, prepare, and serve them. The optimum time to purchase fruits and vegetables is during their season. Try canned or frozen vegetables instead; they are equally nutrient-dense and cost-effective. Each day, you want to consume at least 5 servings of vegetables and 2 servings of fruit. Pick a variety of hues and types.

If you don't particularly enjoy eating fruit or veggies, start out with those that you do. Try preparing, cooking, or serving them in various ways. Additionally, you can cover them up in sauces, minced dishes, or curries.

Fruit and vegetables include vitamins and minerals.

Numerous healthy vitamins and minerals can be found in fruits and vegetables. Numerous these are antioxidants and may lower the risk of developing a variety of diseases:

- A vitamin (beta-carotene)
- Vitamin C
- Vitamin E
- Magnesium
- Zinc
- Phosphorous
- Vitamin B12.
- Homocysteine, a chemical that may be a risk factor for coronary heart disease, may be decreased by folic acid in the blood.

According to research, ingesting these nutrients naturally—in fruits and vegetables—rather than as supplements, is better for your health.

Vegetables and fruits for health

Low in sugar, salt, and fat are fruits and vegetables. They are a wonderful source of dietary fiber, which helps keep you satisfied for longer and help you avoid overeating. A high consumption of fruit and vegetables, along with a balanced, healthy diet and an active lifestyle, can enable you to:

- To lessen obesity and keep a healthy weight
- Reduced cholesterol
- Your blood pressure will drop.

Fruits and vegetables for disease prevention

Antioxidants and phytochemicals, or plant compounds, are found in fruits and vegetables. You may be able to ward off some diseases with the use of these biologically active compounds.

According to scientific studies, eating a lot of fruit and vegetables frequently lowers your risk of developing:

- Diabetes type 2
- Stroke
- Cardiovascular (heart) disease
- Several types of cancer, including bowel, stomach, and throat cancers that develop in later life
- Blood pressure is high (hypertension).

Variety of fruits

Fruit is a plant's sweet, fleshy, and edible component. Typically, it has seeds in it. Fruits are typically consumed fresh, though some can be prepared. They are available in a wide range of hues, forms, and flavors. There are many easily available common fruit varieties, including:

- Pears and apples
- Citrus fruits, including limes, oranges, grapefruits, and mandarins
- Stone fruit, including plums, peaches, apricots, and nectarines
- Bananas and mangoes are tropical and exotic foods.
- Strawberries, raspberries, blueberries, kiwifruit, and passionfruit are among the berries.
- Melons, including rockmelons, honeydew melons, and watermelons.
- Avocados with tomatoes.

Vegetable varieties

Vegetables come in a wide range of variations and can be divided into various biological "families," such as:

- Leafy green – lettuce, spinach and silverbeet
- Cruciferous – cabbage, cauliflower, Brussels sprouts and broccoli
- Marrow – pumpkin, cucumber and zucchini
- Root – potato, sweet potato and yam
- Edible plant stem – celery and asparagus
- allium – onion, garlic and shallot.

Varieties of fruits.

Varieties of vegetable

Fruits and vegetables' colors

Comparable protective chemicals are typically present in foods with similar colors. In order to reap the full variety of health advantages, try to eat a rainbow of vibrant fruits and veggies every day. For instance:

- Food that is red, such as tomatoes and melons. These include lycopene, which is thought to be crucial for preventing heart disease and prostate cancer.

- Green veggies, such as kale and spinach. These have lutein and zeaxanthin, which may help ward off eye diseases associated with aging.

- Foods that are blue or purple, such as blueberries and eggplant. These have anthocyanins, which could shield the body against cancer.

- Foods that are white, like cauliflower. These include sulforaphane and might also offer some cancer protection.

Choosing Fruits and Veggies

Purchase and serve a variety of fruits and vegetables to receive the most nutrition and attractiveness. Choose fresh and high-quality produce that is in season whenever possible. You ought to:

- Eat according to the season; this is how nature ensures that our bodies receive a balanced diet of minerals and phytochemicals.

- Try something new by trying out new dishes and adding fresh produce to your monthly grocery list.

- Put a "rainbow" of colors on your plate (green, white, yellow-orange, blue-purple, and red) to acquire diverse combinations of nutrients.

Tips for healthy fruit and vegetable servings for your family

Serving sizes of fruits and vegetables include, for instance:

- 1/2 cup cooked vegetables, either orange or green (for example, broccoli, spinach, carrots or pumpkin)
- 1/2 cup of cooked dry, canned, or lentils (preferably with no added salt)
- 1 cup of raw or green leafy salad veggies
- 1 medium banana, orange, apple, or pear.
- 2 tiny plums, kiwifruits, or apricots
- 1 cup of fruit, diced or in a can (no added sugar)
- 125ml (12 cup) of fruit juice with no sugar added, only on occasion

30g dried fruit, such as 4 dried apricot halves or 112 teaspoons of sultanas, should only be consumed on rare occasions.

Fruit and vegetables are convenient snack foods that are portable to work or school. For a wholesome, balanced diet, incorporate them into everyone's meals and snacks. Several recommendations are:

- Maintain easily accessible snack-size quantities of fruits and vegetables in your refrigerator.
- Place some fresh fruit on the table or seat.
- Include fruit and vegetables in your favorite family recipes and regular dinners.
- To make your meals more interesting, use a variety of fruit and vegetables for their color and texture.
- Come up with inventive methods to present fruits and veggies. Try preparing, cooking, or serving them in various ways. Additionally, you can cover them up in sauces, minced dishes, or curries.
- Vegetables that are frozen or canned are just as nutrient-dense as those that are fresh, and they also offer convenience and affordability.
- Make small adjustments every day. Consider putting salad on your sandwiches or ordering more vegetables for dinner.

Serving fruits and vegetables in an easy manner includes:

- salads of fruits and vegetables
- stir-fries with vegetables or meat and vegetables
- fruit and vegetable juices
- veggie soups
- Fruits in a snack pack, in stewed or canned form, or dried.

Fruit juice shouldn't be consumed in excess because fresh fruit has more nutrients than fruit juice. It also has a lot of sugars in it. Despite being "natural," these sugars are not necessarily good for your health. Have a glass of water and some fruit instead.

Cooking and preparing fruit and veggies

Despite certain varieties being eaten raw, vegetables are frequently prepared. Some minerals and phytochemicals in plant-based foods can be harmed by cooking and processing.

- To get the most out of your fruit and veggies, try these tips:
- If possible, consume raw fruits and vegetables.
- Try making smoothies with pureed fruit or vegetables.
- To prevent bruising when cutting fresh fruit, use a sharp knife.
- Vegetables should only have their edible sections removed; occasionally, the finest nutrients can be found in the skin, the area just beneath the skin, or the leaves.
- Use mono-unsaturated oils, non-stick cookware, and the stir-fry, grill, microwave, bake, or steam ways to prepare food.
- Avoid overcooking to minimize nutritional loss.
- Replace sour condiments with vegetable pestos, salsas, chutneys, and vinegars when preparing meals.

Cooking food may actually boost some nutrients, including carotenoids. For instance, cooking tomatoes increases their amount of carotenoids, particularly lycopene, which is a good reason to prepare fruits and vegetables in different ways. Spend some time on presentation after you've chopped, cooked, and prepped your fruit and vegetables. If a meal is varied, pleasant on the eye, and tasty, people are more likely to enjoy it.

Meals shared with others typically contain more items from all five food groups. For instance, people frequently claim that they find it too difficult to prepare veggies for themselves. Enjoy your meal at the table without any outside distractions, such as television. Watching television is linked to consuming fewer foods from the five food groups and more discretionary foods, such as takeout or convenience foods. Additionally, it makes it far more challenging to recognize and act upon our bodies' signals of hunger and fullness (satiety).

CHAPTER 6

BENEFITS OF HEALTHY EATING

Here is all the encouragement you need to keep eating well.

Let's start talking about the topic right away.

1. More Economically Sound

Spend substantially less money when you eat healthfully. You notice a significant decrease in your grocery costs, and if you already have credit card debt, you avoid adding to it. Additionally, you save a ton of money on all the medical costs you would incur if a problem resulting from your eating binges arises.

2. Your health improves

Even if we wrote a whole library of books about the health benefits of eating properly, they wouldn't exactly address what benefits actually exist. The main benefit is that you have more control over your weight. By eating properly, you also ensure that your metabolic processes continue to run smoothly, particularly those of your digestive and immunological systems. You are also protected from a variety of chronic ailments, including diabetes and cardiovascular conditions including coronary artery disease and high blood pressure.

3. Your body contains less toxins.

Nowadays, a lot of meals are poisonous due to the synthetic chemicals they contain. One of the fundamental tenets of eating right is that you shouldn't consume any man-made foods, so when you try to eat properly, you are significantly less likely to introduce these poisons into your body.

In addition, cutting back on vices like smoking and drunkenness will be possible if you eat less. A beer nearly always signifies a night out with the guys. You won't crave the beer as much if you eat less. Similar to this, you won't want to smoke one (or more) cigarettes after every meal as is usual.

4. A more active lifestyle

You'll discover that you can function much more effectively when you eat better. You can live a more productive life by getting more exercise, traveling, playing, and working. That certainly beats being a slob and spending the entire day on the couch, doesn't it? Additionally, you are able to spend more time with your friends and loved ones, which unquestionably improves your quality of life.

5. Optimal Social Life

Forget about the "fat fetishism," overweight people don't look good. Weight on the wrong areas of the body is strongly stigmatized in society. Your extra weight can actually hinder your ability to locate a companion. Not only that, but those who have trouble controlling their eating and weight are viewed negatively by society as having trouble controlling their basic desires. There is this kind of psychology, but very few people will talk about it. When you eat properly, you'll notice that these problems go away.

6. Cardiovascular health

By regulating blood pressure and cholesterol levels, a heart-healthy diet full of fruits, vegetables, whole grains, and low-fat dairy can help lower your chance of developing heart disease. A diet high in salt and saturated fats can cause high blood pressure and cholesterol.

Consuming oily fish, such salmon and trout, once a week can also help to reduce your risk of heart disease. Oily fish has a lot of omega-3 fatty acids, which are excellent for the heart.

7. Strong teeth and bones

A diet high in calcium can help prevent bone loss (osteoporosis) brought on by aging and maintain the strength of your teeth and bones.

Dairy products are typically linked to calcium, although you can also receive calcium by eating:

- canned salmon, pilchards, or sardines (with bones)
- dark green produce, like kale and broccoli
- foods with added calcium, such as cereals, fruit juices, and soy products

Make sure to get outside (your body produces vitamin D from the sun) and include lots of foods containing vitamin D in your diet, such as fatty fish and fortified cereals, as vitamin D aids in calcium absorption.

CONCLUSION

There are several well-liked diets available today, but the majority of them are harmful and occasionally even dangerous. This will describe how to avoid unhealthy diets and maintain a healthy, balanced diet for life. Find out how many calories your body needs every day to function. Depending on your metabolism and level of physical activity, this figure may vary greatly. Your daily caloric intake should remain around 2000 calories for men and 1500 calories for women if you're the type of person who gains 10 pounds after just smelling a slice of pizza.

Additionally, your body mass affects this: For naturally bigger people, more calories are recommended, and for smaller people, fewer calories. You may want to boost your daily caloric intake by 1000–2000 calories, a little less for women, if you're the type of person who can eat without gaining weight or you're physically active.

Avoid avoiding greasy foods. For your body to function properly, you must consume fat from food. But it's important to choose the right kinds of fats: The majority of animal fats and a few vegetable oils are high in the LDL (bad) cholesterol-raising kind of fat. Contrary to popular opinion, eating cholesterol doesn't always increase your body's level of cholesterol. Your body will eliminate additional cholesterol if you give it the right resources. You should strive to routinely take monounsaturated fatty acids, which are those tools. Olive oil, almonds, fish oil, and various seed oils are foods high in monounsaturated fatty acids.

Obtain plenty of the proper carbohydrates. Since carbohydrates are your body's primary source of energy, you must consume foods high in them. The secret is to choose the right carbs. Sugar and refined wheat are examples of simple carbohydrates that are rapidly absorbed by the body. Your body responds by releasing massive amounts of insulin to combat the overload, which causes a form of glucose overload. In addition to harming your heart, too much insulin also promotes weight growth.

Eat a lot of carbohydrates, but choose foods like whole grain flour, vegetables, oats, and unprocessed grains that the body can digest slowly.

 Make eating slowly a habit. It will make you feel full with less calories while preventing overeating and obesity with all of its negative effects.

Obtain enough of water. It improves your skin, awakens you and gives you more energy, and makes you feel fuller so you eat less. You will benefit greatly from reducing your soda use and switching to water.

Provide a treat dinner for yourself. Cheating involves enjoying a food you genuinely love once a week rather than bingeing on all the wrong things once a week. On Sundays, have a few slices of pizza, and on Saturdays, eat a giant slice of double chocolate cake. This treat meal is beneficial to your health in several ways and will help you stick to your new diet. Birthdays in the family and other special events are considered cheat meals.

Eat larger meals first thing in the morning. As the evening wears on, your metabolism slows down and becomes less effective at breaking down meals. That means your body won't absorb as many nutrients from the meal and more of the energy included in the food will be stored as fat. Try eating a large meal for lunch, a medium-sized meal for dinner, and a small meal for breakfast. Better still, try eating 4-6 small meals throughout the course of the day.

Printed in Great Britain
by Amazon